A Day in Indigenous Bugwere Community

Preserved Old Ways of African Society

Copyright © Comfort Onyee, 2022

The right of Comfort Onyee to be identified as the author of this work has been asserted in

accordance with Section 78 of the Copyright, Designs and Patents Act 1988.

This book is published by RBKCL Publishing Ltd Link Flat 12 Hood House, Elmington Estate, Brisbane Street, Southwark, LONDON SE5 7QN. www.rbkcl.co.uk

A CIP record for this book is available from the British Library

ISBN 978-1-7396974-9-5

Declaration

All trademarks, design rights, copyrights, registered names, the logo, the symbols, the references, sites in this book remain property of their respective owners. The author reserves the right to change the focus of the book; shut down; sell; and or change the terms of use at any time as deemed appropriate by the Brainchild; the author reserves the right to update additional evidence if needed. This additional evidence may be in the form of newly revealed historical artefacts, and or new observations, statistics etc. The author reserves the right to the inputs, to delete and or make changes required at any time deemed appropriate

To the revered one –

African Rituals –

Ancient Recitation /Htp. di. nsw.t/

Contents

Abbreviations .... page 7

Transliteration .... page 9

Prefix .... page 13

Introduction .... Page 14

Content .... page 21

Literature .... page 36

Discussion... page 54

The way forward .... page 110

Key words .... page 116

Suffix .... page 117

About the author page118

Abbreviations

ARFSD;	Africa Regional Forum for Sustainable Development
AIIF;	Africa Innovation and Investments Forum
AUC;	African Union Commission.
AVwDHA; Org	Added Value with Diaspora Home-Away.
BC;	Before Christ
BCOR;	Bugwere Community Out-Reach.Org.
CCD-X	Climatic Change and Development – 10th Conference held in Africa.
DSD;	Division for Sustainable Development Goals
EASG;	Education Academic Stakeholder Group
HLPF;	High Level Political Forum
HR;	Human Rights
OMCOR;	Old Mosh Community Out-Reach

MGoS;	Major Groups and other Stakeholders in SDGs
NGO;	Not Government Organization
PBLLRA;	Principles of Building Local Libraries in Rural Africa
RBK21;	Re-Birth of Knowledge in the 21st century
BKSDG2030;	Re-Birth of Knowledge in the Era of SDG2030
SDG;	Sustainable Development Goals
UNESCO;	United Nations Educational, Scientific and Cultural Organization's International World Heritage program.
UN;	United Nations
WHO;	World Health Organization?

Transliteration from Mother Language in Ancient Africa to English ...

/ii. ti. m. Htp/; Welcome in peace.

/Htp di nsw.t/; Opening prayer/ Offering Formula/ Recitation in Ranykemet language at an opening of an event or ceremony. The length and or concept of the /Htp di nsw.t/ depends on the event.

/Dd mdw in
ink mAt Ra/; Words spoken by I/me daughter of Ra

/Hwt. Ka. Ptah/; House of all / Soul of Ptah

/Ka/; the Soul, the Spirit

/Km.t/; Black ↔ Coal ↔ Kemet ↔ black Land and everything on there.

/nTr/; God – Sun

/Netcheru/;	God/ Life ↔ infinite ↔ existence, existence cannot exist yet deny the existence of exist.
/Mdw/;	Words
/Prt.ptah/;	House of Words, House for all, House of Rulership ...
/Ra/;	using the Gardiner codes, we look in the Vygus dictionary and find N5 is /Ra = Sun or det. hrw, "day" or sw, "day" or N5 Det sun ↔ times ↔ Sun-God ↔ Enlightenment.
/sbA.t/;	love of wisdom.
/Snt/;	Sister
/Sn/;	Brother
/sn.wr/;	Older brother/ elderly man
/sn.t wr.t/;	Older sister/ elderly woman
/Shm.m. Htp/;	Travel in peace.
/sSw/;	Scribe ↔ write. sSw mdw nTr; Scribe of Divine Words of Netcheru.

Recitation is –

Rituals –/Htp. di. nsw.t/

Indigenous Bugwere give thanks and prayer to their Kibbumba the creator before cutting into the Earth to sow and plant – see below.

Spiritual Sowing Basket, in the basket is millet grain, millet crop is held in Sacred position, Indigenous Bugwere believe it is immoral to eat new harvested millet before annual food festival is held.

Spiritual sowing and planting hoes. Firstly, praise and thanks shall be to Kibbumba the creator before cutting into the Earth to sow and plant.

Prefix

- What is the incentive of writing a book; "A Day in Indigenous Bugwere"?
- What is the goal?

The incentives of "A Day in Indigenous Bugwere" is inspired from "ideologies" and or philosophizing of Indigenous Bugwere; Saga Philosophy; in other words; Bugwere communal knowledge; a practice passed down in traditional libraries also known as oral literature in Indigenous Bugwere.

Bugwere is one of the youngest communities of Africa descendance, and that leads to immediate questions like, what is communal knowledge of Bugwere, because what qualifies a community is their communal knowledge, and how is Indigenous Bugwere ideology in comparison with African sister communities etc.

The goal is to pass down Indigenous Bugwere Philosophizing basing on traditional libraries to modern era. For I believe at most by 2050 there will hardly be a Bugwere traditional library ...

Introduction

/Htp/ – Mirembe – Aman – Peace –
Indigenous Bugwere Greets you –

Owe'ikka:	Oo koizeyo, koizeyo.
Sage:	Koizeyo tuliyo.
Owe'ikka:	Oo koizeyo, koizeyo.
Sage:	Koizeyo tuliyo.
Sage:	Ale mwisukeyo ebiseera e'byo.
Owe'ikka:	Ummmm mwena o'kutusabira.
Sage:	Ale mwisukeyo ebiseera e'byo.
Owei'kka:	Ummmm mwena o'kutusabira.
Sage:	Oo eisanyu, eisanyu.
Owe'ikka:	Eisanyu lya njita.
Sage:	Oo eisanyu, eisanyu.
Owe'ikka:	Eisanyu lya njita.
Sage:	Nagabenga.
Owe'ikka:	Owe.
Sage:	Nagabenga iwe

Owe'kka:	Owe
Sage:	Nagabenga okeizera ...

Owe'ikka:	Intuka mubugeni, intuka mubugeni banange intuka mubugeni ...

Sage:	Nagabenga okeizera, o'yibbireku enyama?
Owe'ikka:	Ndi njibba kintu banange neyuna lugendo, omwoyo gwagonere eyo nga gukuulya bukuuli …

Sage:	Nagabenga okezera.
Owe'ikka:	Ndi njibba kintu banange neyuna lugendo.

Akasana kanene, uhmmm, mwena mukabone. Ebigere byange binu tibitaka mwisana. Mulimu o'buntu budi obukudulya omu bigere.

Sage;	Gaba gambuuza?
Owe'ikka;	Mmmmmm mubbaire mwatuuca.

Mwize mundole
agambuuza gademba
ganjita ...

Sage;   Nagabengaah, iwe oli
             munyoomi.

             Ekintu ec'eika, iiwe oleeta
             mubugeni?

Owe'ikka;   Munkubbiremu ekyo,
             omunwa tilugali, ebyo
             tubireke. ...

Owe'ikka;   Onkoko waiswe
             omusesere, mwabe
             muleete.

Owe'ikka;   Ombuli waiswe owo
             mulevu, yena tubbaage.

Sage;   Ummmmmmm.
Sage;   Omutwe, ebigere ebyo
             badyake.

Sage;   Onanyere e ika.
Owe'ikka;   Yeriire.
Sage;   Onanyere e ika.
The Verdict; Ye r i i r e e e e ... y e r i i
             r e e ...
             Yerireeeeeeeeh ...

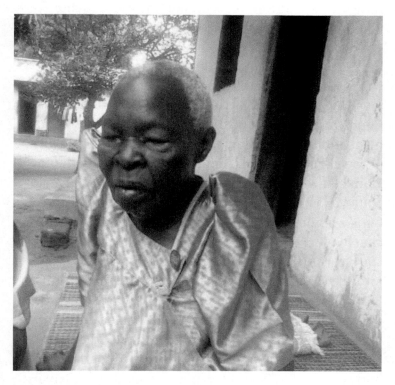

Traditional Libraries in Indigenous Bugwere –

Indigenous Bugwere communal libraries is where you find guide of the ideologies of the community. Take for example organizing in Indigenous Bugwere begins with family home under their clan unique value of "Taboo, Clan names, land ownership; a wealthy" ... The family homes belong with their clan Courtyard(s), Courtyard is where Clan Elders were born and still live. Clan leaders are chosen from any of the clan courtyards. Clan Leaders can never come from elsewhere other than from one of the clan courtyards, basically that is to say the courtyards and family homes must belong with their clan. Therefore, clan leaders are chosen from one of the clan courtyards, by Elders in the clan. Bugwere is Oral Literature, also known as Community of Traditional Libraries, whereby Artefacts like Bugwere ideologies and philosophizing has been limited to oral literature only, by the colonial school curriculum ... the Clan Drum Assemblies *"Mubaala"* are recorded in oral literature only. The fables and idioms. The Courtyard Shrine: *"Kirolero"* these too are still being recorded in traditional libraries only. The ceremonial animals' skins, the animal tails, the Initiation sticks, ceremonial copper metals, all these Indigenous

Bugwere Culture Values in the period of our lives remain recorded in communal libraries only. And things like copper metal is commonly a symbol of divinity in Bugwere, nonetheless, all these artefacts remain limited to oral literature in the communal libraries. Consequently, the goal of "A Day in Indigenous Bugwere" is wakeup call in Indigenous communal knowledge. In indigenous Bugwere, the Elders are held high up as an embodiment of wisdom and justifiably, so.

Growing up in the 1960s – 1980s, I remember this phrase; "Ask the elders"; whenever we needed answer to life's issues, someone would retort, "go ask the old wise woman", or go ask the wise old man. And sure, enough the elders provided satisfactory answers to the numerous questions in the minds of the youths. The elders may sometimes use fables and or Idioms to explain the answer(s) better.

"Elders" is an affectionate name that refers to any elderly individual usually past the age of about 75. Usually in that age, they have become Great Grandparents who are keepers of communal knowledge. Something that is striking about our Elders is their humanity. They never flaunt their knowledge. And when they did not know the answer, they admitted it so and told us to go look for the answers from this or that place, bring back the information found out; for it is wise to share such information.

Interestingly, through fables and idioms, traditional libraries share knowledge life none than human life, e.g. The hyena is used as symbol of wisdom; that the hyena is one of the clever animals in the jungle, where the saying goes; "as clever as a hyena". But is that all? No, there is another animal in the jungle that preys on the hyena. In other words, with all its cleverness there is an animal that outsmarts the hyena.

Lesson to learn: no man is an Island of knowledge, and in other words, no one is custodian of knowledge, and Indigenous Bugwere is like that; they follow Ancestral African clan organizing for political economy, and moral beliefs ...

Content

Time Management in Bugwere

LUGWERE	MEANING	ENGLISH
Nankungu	Time of much dust	January
Naisiga	Time of sowing especially millet	February
Naizuba	Time of weeding	March
Gatonya	Time of much rain	April
Nanzala	Time of scarcity of food	May
Nairima	Time of serious hoeing/digging	June
Naikesa	Time of harvesting mainly millet	July
Nampindi	Time of sowing peas	August
Musambya	Time of sporadic rain; short planting season	September
Naaya	Time of picking especially cotton	October
Najuuli	Beginning of second dry season	November
Ndobooli	dry season intensity	December

Chant of movements and struggles –

Sage;	Onyonyo omutono.
Community;	Nzeremba, onyonyi, onyonyo omutono nzeremba.
Sage;	Onyonyo omutono.
Community;	Nzeremba, onyonyi, onyonyo omutono nzeremba
Sage;	Onyonyi oyooooooo.
Community;	Nzeremba, aaaaaaaaa, Nzeremba.
Sage;	Onkodoleeeeeeeeeee.
Community;	Nzeremba, aaaaaaaaa, nzeremba
Sage;	Onyonyo omutono
Community;	Nzeremba, onyonyi, onyonyo omutono nzeremba.
Sage:	Onyonyo omutono.
Community;	Nzeremba, onyonyi, onyonyo omutono nzeremba.
Sage;	Ke kyussa kyussaaaaaaaaaaaaaaaaaa aaaa …

Community;	Nzeremba, onyonyi, omutono nzeremba.
Sage;	Ka sonya banna be ...
Community;	Nzeremba, aaaaaaaa, Nzeremba.
Community;	Ohhh, banange e kyenkoba.
Sage;	Hmmmmm ...
Community;	Twabe tu kalete.
Sage;	Hmmmmm ...
Community	Kaisi tukadunde.
Sage;	Hmmmmm ,
Community;	Kaisi tukalire?
Sage;	Hmmmmm ...
Community;	Oku bwitta okuwoma ...
Sage;	Oh nzeremba ...
Community;	Nzeremba, nzeremba aaaaaaaaa Nzeremba.
Sage;	O'nkodoleee ...
Community;	Nzeremba aaaaaaa, nzeremba ...
Sage;	O'nyony'iooooo
Community;	Nzerembaa aaaa, nzeremba ...
Community;	Nzeremba, onyonyi, omutono Nzeremba ...
Sage;	Onyonyo omutono ...
Community;	Nzeremba, onyonyi, omutono Nzeremba ...

Sage;	Onyonyo omutono …
Community;	Nzeremba, onyonyi, omutono nzeremba.
Sage;	Onyonyo omutono …
Community;	Nzeremba, onyonyi, omutono nzeremba.
Community;	Oooooo banange ekindi te …
Sage;	Hmmmm …
Community;	Kawoma kokye …
Sage;	Hmmmm.
Community;	Kaisi otumunyu …
Sage;	Hmmmm …
Community;	Okubwitta okuwoma …
Sage;	Oo'nzerembaah …
Community;	Nzerembaa aaaaaa Nzeremba …
Sage;	Onyoyi ooyoooh …
Community;	Nzerembaa aaaaaaa nzeremba.
Sage;	Onyonyo omutono. …
Community;	Nzeremba, onyonyi, omutono nzeremba.
Sage;	Onyonyi mutono …
Community;	Nzeremba, onyonyi, omutono Nzeremba ….
Sage;	Onanyere eika.
Community;	Yelilre eeeee yelire.
Sage;	Onanyere eika.

Community;	Yelilre eeeee yelire.
Sage;	Onyonyi oyooooooo.
Community;	Nzeremba, aaaaaaaaa, Nzeremba ...
Sage;	Onkodoleeeeeeeeeeeee ...
Community;	Nzeremba, aaaaaaaaa, Nzeremba.
Sage;	Ooo... nyonyi... oyooooooo.
Verdict;	Nzerembaaaaaa haaaaa. Nzerembaaaaaaaaaah ...

Indigenous Bugwere ideologies –

Meanwhile the elders are the communal libraries held high up as an embodiment of wisdom what are the young and adult ages good at?

To argue what the young and adult ages are good at, in Indigenous Bugwere, you will need an introduction to the Time Management Plan, (see page 21) above.

But also, you will need to study Chants written in this book. You will soon learn Sage philosophy of Indigenous by also studying the communal chants. In Indigenous people. In indigenous Bugwere, the hour of day begins from Cockcrow to Noonday, to Evening Folklore Time, to the Hour of quiet and sleep, and into cockcrow. And that gives you 5 hours of day, not 24 hours of day. In Indigenous Bugwere traditional home(s) are the primary units and at the bottom of a clan hierarchy.

Above the family home(s) in clan hierarchy sits the Courtyard. The courtyard is home of family lineage: Elders ↔ great grandfather ↔ grandfather father ↔ father and down to the children. Elders are normally, head of the courtyard and the family homes in that clan lineage. The eldest fathered the rest. The courtyards choose a clan leader from one of their courtyards to sit as clan-leader. Bugwere Community was a community of clans to clans, ideology until the 21st. century when contemporary Bugwere began to consider re-establish Bugwere into a monarchy.

The young and adult are good at, time management and work, and as you will see below –

A family home is best managed by a husband and his wives following the Time Management plans as shown on page 21 above. Hard working men and their wives earn good names in the clans, and in Bugwere Community at large. The fathers and mothers work hard in all ways and that includes child-up bringing. Work time begins at Cock-craw, family heads take lead in get out of bed to begin day work.

The gardeners, go gardening, the fishermen go fishing, the hunters get up to sharpen and assemble themselves a long side their hunting tools, on the one hand. And on the other hand, the blacksmith might need more sleep, the Journalists/ artists pull-off the bedcovers from their ears to tune in their ears to gather the news and dramas of the day in the Villages.

Somewhere I read; the Luo people of Uganda, at Cockcrow they begin by rolling-up the papyrus mats and hung papyrus mats across the hooks up on the wall in the house before going out to work. Bugwere are not like that. Bagwere simply throw back the coverings, living the papyrus mats as flat as the papyrus mat was used for sleeping over. Indigenous Bagwere hardly roll-up their beddings and put them on the hook, rather, when Bagwere come back home for lunch, is when they bring out the papyrus mats for fresh air, until dusk.

In Indigenous Bugwere all talents and skills are always on the alert, they are always fired up, and ready to go. Now listen to this, it is important – At the cockcrow, the adults get up and walk to work. Nonetheless, should domestic violence begin at cockcrow and after? The village journalists and artists get jobs of that day and put them in the evening news and folksongs. Any domestic violence from cockcrow to the time of the central meal of day. All blame goes to the women. Drown from conclusion that the woman or women are lazy, and that causes domestic violation in the early hours of the day. The woman takes the blame, the man takes the favour. Drawn from the conclusion that, if the woman got out of bed and went straight to work, how else would the man or violet the woman?

In Indigenous Bugwere, any domestic violence after the day's central meal "Dinner", the village journalists, and artists conclude it is the man or men at fault? Drown from the conclusion that the man or men from XXX homes are greedy man or men. These men have been feed, next, they should leave the homes, for the next task and later proceed to town to join in community meetings or simply engage in men-to-men conversation(s) etc. After the central meal, the men need do one of the two, and or both. Either to go to the wilderness or forest to find some building materials to do some repairs in the home, and thereafter, go to town to the men's meetings about communal matters.

Women and children continue with some work and to prepare and cook a light meal "supper". After supper, is followed by quality time for, folktales, folksongs riddles and quiz before bedtime. In indigenous Bugwere meanwhile, study time goes on in homes. In the towns, time is right for the evening news by the journalists and the artists airing news and to let be known where and, in whose home, the domestic violence(s) took place from cockcrow to study time of day.

But the married men yet must round off the town meetings and get home. Now listen to this – In indigenous Bugwere, in the time of quiet and sleep; about 11:00 PM to the cockcrow, the journalists and artists must carefully sort domestic violence, never be put in the evening news, or compose a song about it until the Elders get to the bottom of the matter, some domestic violence of this hour is sensitive matters that could be about sexual weakness of total failure, therefore, it is best left to the elders to deal with it and get to the bottom of the matter.

Indigenous Bugwere Moral Philosophy –

Indigenous Bugwere moral philosophy is from African Spiritual Philosophy. Every courtyard is furnished with a Shrine "Kirolero". Also known as the house for all or meeting place. But besides, Kirolero is also used as a place of worship.

Copper metal –

Copper is the metal of divinity in many African myths … Copper metal is also identified with spiritual well-being in body muscles and joints. So, when you see Indigenous Bugwere wearing copper bangles, it is in connection with spiritual belief for wellbeing in mind and fulfilling life's purpose. Copper metal is also used as symbolism, of connecting people with their ancestors.

Since copper is metal of the divine, indigenous Bugwere who wear copper bangles, it means they are establishing their direct relationship with the divine and their primacy in the divine order. To this extent, to understand Indigenous Bugwere peculiarities, one must also understand that Bugwere is member community in Bantu peopling from ancient Africa to contemporary Africa. Which is also visible from African ideologies.

In this book pictures will be used to speak for themselves, so that one gets the idea in the picture. If not, Africa Oral literature is systematic in its own ways, so that the user gets the message being communicated, but that also depends on your knowledge about the culture in question, see below –

Healing Rituals lead by Sharman.

The person in white dress looks like she is sitting on her knees, well she is not – she is away from this world, she is on Call in the world of Spirits as a go between the Spirits and with us.

Page 32, in the top picture, the kneeling lady in white is spiritually guarded with these two wearing animal skins, armed with spiritual spears on guard, the person on the knees, to her right is the Sharman to lead us through this Healing Ritual. You must be respectful of Spiritual Beliefs: Deity Malidoma teaches us about African Spirituality in his book; "Rituals": Malidoma Patrice Somé 1997 1997 ...

... Malidoma writes that; after the Spirits realise her or the few who have just returned from the world of higher spirits and back to their human spirits in society, let them be first talk to by those who have gone through Initiation Rites to welcome her or them home, a psychological way, to help them recover psychologically and physically. For it is true, those persons could become traumatized from the experience she or he is waking up from, so, in occasions, the Deities or Sharman must help them to come back to life, may be with surprise but not fear ...

Healing Rituals lead by a Sharman ...
... In Indigenous Bugwere (minus the born-again) Now and then we do Healing Rituals lead by a Sharman as above picture illustrations. In that act,

one or a few of us suddenly will exit us in body spirit for higher spiritual life, and once in the higher spiritual life, they converse with us mystically, yet the conversation with us is about our social problems. and before they higher spirits exit the conversation; they request of our wishes and needs in society. And once all that must be said is said, they set themselves free from the human body, meaning they are now free to come back to us in society.

And this is what Malidoma teaches us that those peoples' minds or souls that enter the world spiritual lives different from spirit of the human body and back to the human spirit, firstly, must be in a private conversation with a deity or Sharman to understand what has just happened to them, before any of us can interact with them. Usually, the elders greet them after the Deity, children should be there to watch and learn only. If any of them is a parent to toddlers, the toddlers must be prevented from jumping into the arms of their parents until the parents have gone through the process of psychological awareness, the time out of their human spirit, to the time back to their human spirit ...

... *"You know the Dagara peoples in West Africa are very smart, they leave all that to only the people who have gone through Initiation rites i.e., the Deities and Sharman the people who learn how to control. And whereby there are many verbal keys like this. For example, there are (is) the one that can make you completely invisible, it can even make you invisible to the camera"* ... **by Malidoma Patrice Somé 2010.**

Ritual; going to the ceremony of thanksgiving, following the harvest season.

Literature

Chant of indigenous Bugwere

Sage;	Kudambanga bumeeri
Community;	Kudambaga bumeeri, zena e'izo nagoya, kudambag bumeeri.
Sage;	Kudambanga bumeeri
Community;	Kudambaga bumeeri, zena e'izo nagoya, kudambag bumeeri.
Sage;	Kudambanga bumeeri
Community;	Kudambaga bumeeri, zena e'izo nagoya, kudambag bumeeri.

The hunger for Bugwere ideology brought us here. Now, the wise thing to do is to compared Indigenous Bugwere ideologies with sister languages and cultures of Africa, regardless of the colonial school curriculum influence on indigenous communities. Indigenous Bugwere history is sister history to indigenous Africa history. Bugwere communal knowledge was brought to Bugwere pastureland mostly by the founding fathers arriving from elsewhere in Ancient African Chieferies and Kingdoms. You will find this knowledge passed down condensed in oral literature.

Religious Beliefs is norm in Indigenous Bugwere whereby they worship Kibbumba the Creator. The man and his wives are the home manager and makers, and their children are Bugwere's future.

In Indigenous Bugwere it is uncommon to have neighbours, because the men are fathers to number of children. When the father turns into grandfather and great grandfather and above, his home becomes family courtyard; or call it the umbrella over his sons' family homes. The family homes need to be under the umbrella known as the courtyard, and a courtyard is not just a courtyard, but the courtyard is the owner of the land on which family homes under that courtyard sit. Such that a whole village could belong to only one clan. Then the same clan cannot be neighbours to her own clan because clan members are known as siblings, they are all siblings in the sense that their Taboo is the same one, therefore they cannot marry into their own clan. They must marry into or from other clans. You will learn that Clan leaders are chosen from their own clan courtyards.

The incentive of "A Day in Bugwere" is A Sage Philosophy or simply put as communal knowledge of a people.

I do not know if the linguists will approve that the word "Saga" come from Ranykemet word /sbA.t/ and that is to say; "the love of knowledge". Indigenous Bugwere language, the word "Saga" means to look for something or look for information narrating to true information history. You will find the word saga in other languages including English language. And you will find the word saga is the same word "Sofia" – Sofia is Greek word meaning love of "knowledge and wisdom" which again comes from the hieroglyph /sbA.t/. the word "Sofia" is called "Sonja" in Norwegian – Germanic.

Indigenous Bugwere Courtyard is complete assembly of Elders, the Courtyard Shrine, family homes, and the children to guarantee Indigenous Bugwere the future. In Indigenous Bugwere the courtyard shrine is termed; "Kirolero"; and the word Kirolero comes from the idea of Ancient Africa /Hwt. Ka. Ptah/ or /Prt. Ptah/; meaning House for all; House of Rulership House of Words ...

Kirolero ideas is also spread everywhere on the Africa continent and in the World of the period of our lives and as you will see here to follow –

Indigenous Bugwere Man; his wives with their title in family affairs –

Title	Meaning
1st. wife's Title is: Muyolaikoke	Niye e yatembwire e Kidala on iteye wa bana era niye ayinzza okukikila abakaire oku lugga. Niye ayoola eikoke o kuluuga nga emikolo gibwoile.
2nd. Wife;s Title is: Kabejja or Kamedde	Niye omukali wokubiri, ayila oku Muyola ikoke. Akola e mikolo gya Muyola ikoke nga abulawo.
Kanyali wa bana Kayendeke (kutaka bana)	Yabbanga musa ino omukudunda omaido ekinamuna kaisi omusaiza namutaka ino
Nawende/ Kayezyaki	Yaali mutake ino, niye akwata e nsada yo mukulu, niye a yaba no mukulu okumikolo.
Mudondo/ Konola/ Katengeke	Yaali musumbi eera ng'adendemulira nakimo Konola = Yaali mukoni w'obulo
Nabitetera Katengeke	Yaali mwanilizi wa bageni Yaali mubisi w'ebiseke

The Titles normally from the 1ˢᵗ. wife – 4ᵗʰ wife must be Customary. The wives from 5ᵗʰ and above, normally are about individual character description as here below –

- Muwugumya ... *Yakungiryanga*
- Nawawe ... T*iyalimanga, yasiibanga waawe*
- Tindinamukali ... T*iyatakanga abantu*
- Sumbaatala ... *Aasumbanga batala*
- Namunobe ... *Yaali amaite aati niiye omunobe/atatakibwa obweyayabanga ewaawe, yaiririranga*

In indigenous Bugwere the life of the polygamist and his wives is remarkable, there is order following the wives' titles and position in the family home. divorce in Indigenous Bugwere is normal, and there is protocol to follow how to divorce responsively, if need be; it is considered irresponsible of man and his wives' divorce during sowing and planting season. Because it is work time, where culturally educated people know better than to course domestic violence in work time. Control of domestic violence at any time of day comes from this sense.

Indigenous Bugwere Political economy –

Earlier above the question was put forward that; if the Enders are the community libraries, what are the young adults and children good at?

This question can father be well answered taking the example from the "family home" husband and his wives are the state manager and home makers taking Bugwere Time Management seriously.

The covenant of a husband ↔ his wives and their children shall be understood as the political economy at clan level, to exchange or barter at the clan-to-clan levels is political economy in Indigenous Bugwere.

Divorce is acceptable from mid-November to end of December because at that time of the year, there is time for social activities like exchanging friendship visits, settling conflicts, settling disagreements, and disputes in the community. But if a wife divorces during planting and sowing seasons, the husband must find a clever way to go bring his wife back home, and it will be very easy because her parents are equally busy to waste time on a woman who lost truck of community Time Management Plan.

Traditional family home –

Papyrus, pythons, and a good night's sleep! Papyrus, pythons and a good night's sleep! | Amigos Worldwide

The above photo gives you a snapshot into the reality of bedtime in Indigenous Bugwere. A simple papyrus mat covers the hard floor on which Indigenous Bugwere sleep, usually covering themselves with an old bedsheet for warmth. Papyrus is a plant which grows wildly in swampy areas in Uganda. It's mostly associated with writing in ancient Egyptian times but is widely used across the world: even the English word paper originates from the word papyrus!

Papyrus has many uses, and that includes Indigenous Bugwere wrap the dead bodies in papyrus mats and then put the body in the grave. But not only, though the major one in Indigenous Bugwere is making mats for both children and adults to sleep on, not only, sometimes the papyrus is used to cover ourselves at night, determined by the state of "a" family home economy status. Papyrus stalks are bound together using a twined sisal rope to make mats like the one you see above. These stalks are by no means easy to get a hold of it requires heading to the swamp and often walking long distances under the scorching sun. It is not unusual to meet huge cobra snakes or pythons in these swamps as these are their territories! This game of chance is for the courageous. For the less brave, a mat can be purchased ready-made but will set you back around UGX 5000 (approximately £1). For most to earn this kind of money in rural Uganda, it would mean a whole day's wages, usually from digging land for 6-8 hours non-stop in the heat...really hard work!

During the night, the papyrus mat is spread on the floor for children to sleep on. In most homes, the mat is shared depending on the number of children in the home, often there can be up to 6 children all sleeping on 1 mat! It will always be a cold night's sleep as the mat provides very little insulation from the ground and the thin sheet is barely enough to keep the children warm from the coolness of the night. It really is a never-ending cycle of broken sleep. So how can we make a difference? Papyrus, pythons and a good night's sleep! | Amigos Worldwide

Indigenous Bugwere Communal Knowledge –

Babutidi in *"Bantu Migration and Settlement,"* in *Laman's Kongo Cultural Collection,* (20,000 pp. microfilm, Lidingo, Sweden, 1914. Film No. 1, Cahier XVIII/13), goes on to state:

"A long time ago in antiquity, people did not exist in this Lower-Congo; they come from the north of the country. There also, in the north, people came from far off north, the very north of **Kayinga**. Kayinga is the name of the country [region] where lived our ancestors in antiquity...There they already knew how to weave the cloths they wore, forge hoes and knives that they used. The main reason for their coming in this country [area] was the famine that hit Kayinga. For many years the drought reigned; crops and fruit trees they planted dried up. They suffered a lot for this. Unable to support the suffering they said to each other: "Let's go to Banda-Mputu [Let's pass through the dense forest, the unbreakable wall] and organize chieftaincies, because we have a lot of hunger up here." So they agreed: "Let's go."

In the past, two chieftaincies ruled this part of the world [region]. When people escaped from the north of Kayinga, they separated on their way; some crossed the Nzadi [Congo river], these are people who live in the Nsundi area [the left shore of Nzadi] and others are those who live on the Simu-Kongo [the right shore of the Nzadi]."

Following both Elder Mukume on a'bo Bwiisonkere lore passed down the book writer hereby and following to the text of reference *(20,000 pp. microfilm Lidingo, Sweden, 1914. Film No. 1, Cahier XVIII/13) to Lower Kongo – "Wa-set"* ... the history of Bugwere Community dates to the last "African peopling on the move" out of Abyssinia to penetrate interior Africa; North, West, Central Africa, South Africa, and East Africa forth and back. It is said the earliest people who established Bugwere community arrived in sub-sets of clan members breaking off from their older clans based in Abyssinia and elsewhere in Africa. It is further said that the earliest settlers where Balalaka Clan and Nagwere Kimaadu (Balangila) Clan. The Balalaka Clan settled at present day Busetta and up to Kadama.

Nagwere Kimaadu (Balangila) Clan settled in Budaka up to Naboa, that way Bugwere community was established. Sooner, Basikwe clan arrived and settled at Naboa up to Jami ... Naboa – Jami of the time then, covered the area from present day Naboa to present day Nasenyi – Mbale.

The next clan to arrive was the Bakomolo clan, who settled in Iki-iki. More people arrived on Bugwere pastureland either individually or in smaller numbers; too small to be recognized as a clan. So, for the people who arrived as individuals or in small numbers, either became accepted in the existing clans or formed their own clans. some were obliged to become part of the existing clans.

To belong in a clan is norm, living in clans play significant roles in the social economy of Indigenous Bugwere But what is peculiar about indigenous Bugwere? Here it must be clear that the peopling of Bugwere arrived and settled on Bugwere pastureland, bringing with them Culture, language, food crops. From Africa ancestry, Indigenous Bugwere carried with them Rituals of Thanksgiving and Praise to Kibbumba the Creator. For indigenous Bugwere it is Ritual to Give Thanks and Praise to Kibbumba the Creator before cutting into the Earth to sow and plant. In Indigenous Bugwere, following seasonal harvest it is ritual to give thanks and praise to Kibbumba the creator for crop harvest – in Ritual –

- Libation Pour, to our ancestors from who we learn.
- Libation Pour for our daily struggles
- Libation pour for the youths who carry our promise for tomorrow.

Indigenous Bugwere believe in next life and carry the belief that the dead shall be buried facing the West or where the Sun sets –

> *reference; A quest to the history of Bugwere: Comfort Onyee 2021 revised 2022 and Introduction2 A'bo Bwiisonkere Clan: Comfort Onyee 2022".*

In indigenous Bugwere, it is Moral to setup a Shrine "Kirolero" in the centre of the courtyard. The Kirolero is also known as the house of assembly for all. And with "all" in African sense, refer to the humans in this life; the Ancestors in next life, as well as the Spirits in everything, and that is; the animalia, minerals, metals, the vegetative, the still and everything else.

In Africa history sense, the structure of houses for "all" is called –

- Kirolero;   Indigenous Bugwere
- Tukul;   South Sudan
- Kgotla;   Setswana in Southern Africa
- Toguna;   Dogon people in West Africa
- Temple;   In Ancient Africa
- Temple;   in the Abrahamic civilizations

And as it will be revealed in the Discussion chapter to follow.

Moreover, it is interesting that in history, humans have been compelled to find God throughout history, and to me, the ingrained understanding of God dates to early man in Africa, and then spread throughout all human civilization.

The history of indigenous Bugwere in indigenous Africa history.

Until now you have been looking at Indigenous Bugwere on their native land, so, where or when does Indigenous Bugwere meet the rest of Africa and World?

Short answer –

Indigenous Bugwere is a Bantu agrarian culture, where you know Bantu are date to Early man in Ancient Africa.

Ancient Africa is where Early Man Lived for very long time, and in that long time early man gradually created civilizations and advanced to modern civilizations as you know so in the period of our lives.

In the era of Early man in Africa, created African Spirituality from philosophizing. It was earlier mentioned in the chapters above; how indigenous Bugwere practice religion and beliefs. Please, find on page 21 is Bugwere Annual Calendar Year. The harvest season fall in July and that means the community has been busy since the sowing and planting season to the harvest season, followed by Praise and Thanksgiving Rituals. Normally, that is once more followed by a short planting and sowing season until early November. The rest of the year some of the men are likely to go on expeditions near and far in saga for information and new knowledge.

Other than the above mentioned, throughout the years Businessmen from near and far keep bringing information services and merchandise to Bugwere for barter and in trade. So, Indigenous Bugwere was never isolated from sister communities in Africa and the rest of the world.

Long answer –

Living in the 21st. century, is re-birth of knowledge and, one of the questions that should ring a bell in your mind is, why do you hear of the principle –

"Africa Cradle of Civilization" nonetheless, this is not taught in your school curriculum?

In the 21st century, the way you look at indigenous African must be accompanied with knowledge of where African people are coming from, and why. Living in the 21st century, most likely you are aware of education injustices in the period of our lives. So, to learn a people's history, with regards, you need to take away the dark cloud called colonial school curriculum, so you can see the historical patterns from Africa cradle of civilization to the 21st. century; take for example indigenous Africa agriculture, agriculture pattern in the past was in range of varieties, and that included barter and trade. That was political economy proper, that was the basis in African economy then, and now.

Africa's Strength and Power was understood from African Spiritual Philosophy. African Spirituality guided Ancient Africa strength and confidence in society until 2 000 BCA. When Africa's neighbours of the Mediterranean saw what was going on in Africa Nile Valley, they got up to go there in Africa in hunger for knowledge. And indeed, these neighbours were received in African spiritual morals. Contemporary Africa continues to receive foreigners in African spirit. However, mingling with foreigners both in Ancient Africa civilization and contemporary Africa, as earlier above mentioned, the foreigners first arrived as students and good will tradesmen. But they sooner turned into invaders; they took advantage of African Spiritual morals and hospitality, slowly African civilization declined. As the invaders saw it, Moral Philosophy had become too simplified to handle man in quest for self-rule. Even when one comes to learn the Law, in certain situations, some Laws must decline to let other law precede. Take for example the law forbids us to steal, and to take your own life. but in real hard times of famine and hunger, you can steal to save life.

Another cause of the fall of Africa empire was "Pluralism"— As opposed to diversity, which brings people together based on common interests and doctrine, pluralism recognizes the strength in differences. Pluralism facilitates flexibility, which enables one to view the world through other people's points of view. Politically, this enhances togetherness and friendship ... but in Africa's cause this was not the case, because Africa's pluralism then or now, both pluralisms point out invaders and or colonial minds not interested in African togetherness and friendship, caused African language diversity to go against each other.

But besides, there were also natural disasters like draughts that caused African peopling to move round and about for want of greener pasture in the continent see fig on page 45 "reference *(20,000 pp. microfilm Lidingo, Sweden, 1914. Film No. 1, Cahier XVIII/13) to Lower Kongo – "Wa-set"*. African peopling on the move was mentioned in the chapters ahead, whereby it was made clear, founding fathers of Bugwere community, began with African peopling on the move from Abyssinia to interior Africa.

Ancient Africa Knowledge –

Sobonfu Somé is a renowned, respected teacher and mentor in the world, Sobonfu Somé is one of the first and **foremost voices of African spirituality** to come to the West. Somé was born in Dano, Burkina Faso, a remote West African village with a population of about two hundred people. Dano has preserved the old ways of African village life, with family structures, spiritual practices, and methods of living that have been in place for more than ten thousand years.

In her book title, "The Spirit of Intimacy", Sobonfu Somé distils the ancient teachings and wisdom of her native village to give insight into the nature of intimate relationships. Sobonfu Some generously applies the subtle knowledge from her West African culture to this one. Simply and beautifully, she reveals the role of spirit in every marriage, friendship, relationship, and community. She shares ancient ways to make our intimate lives more fulfilling and secure and offers powerful insights into the "illusion of romance," divorce, and loss. Her important and fascinating lessons from the heart include the sacred meaning of pleasure, preparing a ritual space for intimacy, and the connection between sex and spirituality. Her ideas are intuitively persuasive, provocative, and healing and supported by sound practical advice, along with specific rituals and ceremonies based on those used for thousands of years. With Sobonfu Somé books, the spiritual insights of indigenous Africa take their place beyond those of native America, Europe, and native Asia moreover, important information in the period of our lives in the 21st. century.

Discussion

Chant to a Hero –

Sage:	Nankololo a kankada.
community:	Akankadira banabe.
sage:	Nankololo a kankada.
Community:	Akankadira banabe?
Sage:	Musaki oisukeyo.
Community:	Ogemanga oti yafera yo?
Sage:	Mwabbi oisukeyo
Community:	Ogemanga oti yafera yo? Manssa

Drums only; *Ahaa, ahaa, ahaa...*

Ngaifire obwire, balindika bwire. Ngaifire emisanna, balindika missan. Intensify Manssa Drum Manssa

Drums only; ahaa, ahaa, ahaa...

Chants are very important in Oral literature. Chants are also the community libraries ...

In the 21st century, looking at Bugwere Time Management on page 21 above, one is left to wonder why agriculture is not working for Bugwere if

Africans are Agrarians by Trade or by Ancestry. Why is domestic economy not working for Africa in general?

Short answer –

The SDG2030 have taken it upon them to research and come up with solutions, see below –

Tenth Conference on Climate Change and Development in Africa (CCDA-X), 24 to 28 Oct. 2022, Windhoek, Namibia

CCD-X; Green Grow Opportunity we want –

In the 21st century you are living the era of Project managements where almost all are collaborating using small or big organizations. Take for example AVwDHA.Org., a small unit of Africa in the Diaspora based in both Oslo Norway and Southwark London in United Kingdom these also are participating in the CCD-X and here what was suggested by AVwDHA.Org., **Fetching methodology from African Mother Language in Antiquity –**

creates workspaces for all indigenous communities at all levels. Whether one is doing oral literature in native communities only, or, whether one is doing everything from oral literature to read and write literatures. Fetching methodology from mother language in antiquity works for every intelligible individual and or a given community.

The Green Growth Opportunity we want should open the window for Africa-knowledge-of-self as follows ...

Of the green growth opportunity, we want in Africa is to recovery from erased memory of knowledge-of-self about our Ancestral African civilization, there is detailed information in the African artefacts, arts, and crafts we need to go back to, to study them putting on the lenses of Africa Worldview, we need to remove the cloud hiding African History, so that contemporary African history will no longer be distant dream from Ancestral Africa knowledge which still reside in us, passed down condensed in oral literature.

Indigenous Bugwere Husbands and the titles to their wives in home management–

Where does indigenous Bugwere get the idea of polygamists?

Founding fathers of Bugwere community landed on Bugwere pastureland, carried with them culture and wisdom from their Ancestry in Ancient Africa. Indigenous Bugwere Polygamy Date to Ancient African it is believed polygamy came about to address social problems relatable to social problems in the period of our lives." Social problems like during times of war", Communities were often left with more women than men. "If all males stuck to one partner there would be several women without husbands and children without fathers … that is how polygamy also provides a social safety net for women and children, by ensuring that men are held responsible for their relationships, "In this way you have less children born out of wedlock" on the one hand. And on the other hand, Indigenous Bugwere women ask their husband to marry kinswomen from their maiden homes. It is common in Bantu peopling of Africa for a married women to a polygamist, go back to her maiden home to request for permission from her brother to free his daughter and become a co-wife with her. Although they are paternal auntie and niece. A paternal auntie and her niece are encouraged to get married to the same husbands because of want of togetherness in the family, in belief of raising their children within the confines of a family set up.

African idea of polygamist is also to shows an appreciation of Ancient African customs and traditions. Being a man is not about how much money you have; it is all in the communal knowledge. It is about social economy and as earlier mentioned in the literature chapter. The idea of polygamy is also about growing from small population in a community. It is all about taking care of community affairs.

In indigenous Bugwere, the children were trained to call their biological mother "mother." They called the other wives of their father a "mother" followed by their clan or call them mother followed by their ethnicity name, if the mother(s) are not of Bugwere ethnicity.

A day in Indigenous Bugwere starts from cockcrow

In indigenous Bugwere, there are Several healing Rituals – for example there is healing ritual when the

spirits themselves initiate it in the names of names of either *"Walugono spirit", or "Namaddu spirit".* Then there is healing ritual initiated by a people in case of "food and crop scarcity", and or in case of disease and pandemic; illustrated on page 32 and page 35 above, see also page 72 below. On page 35 is food crops and Libation Waters to prepare and assemble to the Ritual of praise and thanksgiving to Kibbumba the Creator following the harvest season.

There are seasonal Rituals such as the sowing and planting seasonal Ritual; before cutting into the Earth to sow and plant, see below – pages 11, 12 above, and 61 – 62 here below.

There is recitation for prosperity, food festival and all the Kibbumba good given things on which the spirits, ancestors and Indigenous Bugwere live.

African Libation Pour Ritual –

At the beginning of sowing and plant season, the hand hoes must be bound with spiritual grass as here below before cutting into the Earth to sow and plant

- Libation Pour to our ancestors from who we learn –
- Libation Pour for our daily struggles –
- Libation Pour for our youths who carry our promise for tomorrow –

The hoes prepared to use in the sowing and planting Ritual.

A Sacred basket for millet sowing and planting rituals.

Indigenous Bugwere give thanks and prayer to their Kibbumba the Creator before cutting into the Earth to sow millet crop. In indigenous Bugwere finger millet Grain is held Sacred. It is immoral to eat new millet harvest before the harvest food festal, to give thanks and praise to Kibbumba the creator.

The pictures below depict Finger millet crop/ grain - millet is food staple in indigenous Bugwere – above all, for Indigenous Bugwere millet crop is Sacred food crop. It is immoral to eat new millet bread and drink new millet beer before the official food festival following the harvest season.

Finger millet domestication –

The history of finger millet crop for food and beverages, date to Ancient Africa times. This is noticeable in African culture how knowledge is passed down condensed in African oral literature. Finger millet was first domesticated in the great

Lakes Region in Ethiopia and Uganda at about 5 000
BCA. Preparing millet grain for food and beverages
remains the same from ancient Africa to
contemporary Africa – see below here –

Grinding finger millet between two stones has been
around from ancient Africa to contemporary Africa.
Above is the picture of grinding millet in both ancient
time and in contemporary Africa.

After noon-day family members make u-turn, gather in the home for the central meal "Dinner". "see below"

Indigenous Bugwere Courtyard is assembled with Husband, his wives, children and grandchildren

Indigenous Africa central meal of day served any time between 3:00 PM – 6:00 PM the men and male youths above 15 years of age eat together in one plate as here above. The wives, the elderly and children sit together.

After the central meal men usually go to town meetings but also to drink millet beer.

Indigenous Bugwere also do believe that millet is Sacred, millet grain should be first served to the spirits and or ancestors, so that the gods and the spirits bless community or society with peace and calm. It is up to community management to guide her people to be in relation with Kibbumba and the spirits. Sobonfu; Teacher and Author, she teaches us that to our ancestors are synonym with spirits.

pleased, the community gets blessings. And that is why all men of the village must show up in town meeting to sit and drink in common pot. Indigenous Bagwere believe drinking in a common pot is unity, and unity is "Community"? And therefore, all men of the village sit around this pot for unity. And as they are drinking, many issues concerning the community are discussed, and solutions are reached at. The meaning of this was mentioned in the content chapter above. the history of finger millet food and beverages is passed down in oral literature and culture of Africa, and as earlier mentioned in indigenous Bugwere, it was earlier mentioned that in the evening, the men go to town for communal meetings, importantly for communal matter and enjoy millet beer along with. Earlie above the journalists and artist where also mentioned. The journalists assemble to break the news. and artists also assemble to sing-along while provoking the dramas of day in the community.

Millet grain falls under up to 10 types of millet the four common types –

1. Finger millet
2. Silver millet
3. Pearl millet
4. Sorghum

You must study Bugwere Time Management table above if you are to study and understand Indigenous Bugwere properly. After the seasonal harvest, each clan in Indigenous Bugwere must arrange a food festival and recitation at the Clan's Shrine to give thanks and Libation Pour to their Kibbumba the Creator, it is Moral it is Spiritual –

What about the time from 11:PM – Cockcrow?

Time betweem11:00 Pm – cockcrow, is reserved time. Some domestic violence of that time must never be put in the evening news or compose a song about it, domestic violence of this hour of the night is sensitive matters i.e., it could concern sexual weakness in marriage, best left to the elders to deal with. Because if it is sexual failure, that is also a signal from the ancestors besides other causes.

Indigenous Bugwere Religion and Beliefs

Indigenous Bugwere is hierarchy of 4 levels. At the bottom level is family home of Husband, his wives, his children, and everything in his home fall under his management. Above family home level is the courtyard. The courtyards are the keepers of the religious beliefs. The Shrines sit on the courtyards. Above the courtyards is the Clan-leader and his cabinet members, who come from one or more courtyards. and at the top is Bugwere Community. The Community can form a parliament *"Lukiko"* and elect political seats and leaders.

Indigenous Bugwere is deeply rooted in Ancient African Agrarian culture and spirituality. And for that matter indigenous Bugwere is more of a spiritual philosophy community. It is important for Africa people to study her ethics so that Africans tell their history properly.

After the harvest of millet grain and other crops, Indigenous Bugwere is keen at going to the Courtyard Shrine to give thanks and praise to the ancestors and Kibbumba for prosperity, for Food and drinks, pray for work and Wealthy. To the Shrine, "**Kirolero**" Indigenous Bugwere will bring food, the harvested

The Kirolero is open 24/7 follow the red arrow above

Indigenous Bugwere Courtyard always furnished with her peoples …

Healing Ritual initiated by a people or initiated by the spirits themselves

Arriving at a praise and thanksgiving ritual with crops, domestic animals, and fish, spiritual herbs, spiritual tools so that Kibbumba and ancestors bless work of the human hand.

E'Bugwere. leero twalila Nyanyi ...

Indigenous Bugwere Cut-Fish in Lake Kyoga Water shed at Kakoli- Jami in Budaka District ...

The picture above is raw agriculture ... fishing in Indigenous Bugwere in the Lake Kyoga water shade – Kakoli Naboa in Budaka District.

Every day at mealtimes and at Lamps tales, in African cultures we either Dine on the open courtyard or sit inside the Kirolero; open 24/7 and please notice that passers-by are welcome dine with and share their folklore with us at the folklore time if they will.

Again, this is proof Indigenous Bugwere is not a peculiar community in Africa, rather, Indigenous

Bugwere prove to be Africa Cradle of Civilization, continuity.

The Kirolero of Indigenous Bugwere is African Ancestral Knowledge passed down condensed in African Oral Literature. Mark you, oral literature comes with the challenge of how to interpret oral knowledge in the absences of the traditional libraries? So, "ask the old woman/ man." The Kirolero is there to accommodate all, Nonetheless, if you enter the Kirolero, mind your manners please. The Dogon people in West Africa insist on discipline once you are in the Togu-na; "House of Words" or "House for all" ... you must remain sited down.

Indigenous Bugwere is African Spirituality community, consequently has in place Deities or Spiritual Priests or Sharman or the people Africanists and take for example, **Deity Malidoma Somé** teaches you leave Spiritual consultation to the people who have gone through African Spiritual Initiation? Those are the people who take lead in Recitations in Initiation Ceremonies. They are Spiritual Consultants they are a Calling in Kibbumba the Creators name, Amen.

Ancient African Ritual – /Htp. di. nsw.t/

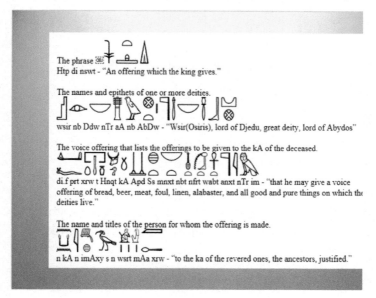

The phrase
Htp di nswt - "An offering which the king gives."

The names and epithets of one or more deities.

wsir nb Ddw nTr aA nb AbDw - "Wsir(Osiris), lord of Djedu, great deity, lord of Abydos"

The voice offering that lists the offerings to be given to the kA of the deceased.

di.f prt xrw t Hnqt kA Apd Ss mnxt nbt nfrt wabt anxt nTr im - "that he may give a voice offering of bread, beer, meat, foul, linen, alabaster, and all good and pure things on which the deities live."

The name and titles of the person for whom the offering is made.

n kA n imAxy s n wsrt mAa xrw - "to the ka of the revered ones, the ancestors, justified."

What you see in the Artefacts of Recitations in contemporary Africa are relatable to recitations in ancient Africa, and that is confirmed by the artefact earlier displayed here above. Good news is scholars who have learnt to read and write the ancient Africa written down language; "Ranykemet" or Hieroglyphs. Then the scholars of Kemet do you favour by transliteration beneath each line of hieroglyphs as shown on page 77 above.

Then the question becomes; "where is Ancient African history in school curriculum"?

In the period of our lives, the 21st. century, African in the Diaspora ask these questions –

January 2018 Racism debate by Johan Galtung Questions and Answers or simply "Q and A" ... you can easily do YOUTUBE review following the link below –

> Jan 2018 Racism debate by Johan Galtung Q and A - YouTube

Kemet community called their language "Ranykemet which means Mouth of Kemet". The language of indigenous Bugwere community in Eastern Uganda is called "Lutumo" which means message of the tongue ... Buganda language in central Uganda is called "*lulimi*" meaning tongue of Buganda ... This is how to

- Indigenous Bugwere has the Kirolero

- Botswana peoples of Southern Africa have the kgotla
- Dogon people have the "Togu-na"
- Abrahamic civilization has the "Temples" or Culture House(s) ...
- Ancient Africa has the "Temples" see below –

All these structures were built on the Principle of African Spirituality. This helps to learn how contemporary Africa culture mirror ancient Africa and ancient Africa culture mirror contemporary Africa culture, see below –

Temple in Ancient Africa; House for All/ House of Words ...

TOGU NA, THE DOGONA 'HOUSE OF WORDS'

TOGU-NA THE DOGON HOUSE OF WORDS

Understanding the Bad News on the African Graduate shoulders –

"African politicians, cultural nationalists and, indeed, historians are left with two ambiguous legacies and as for Africa Historians, they have at least a double task. Africa must free themselves from the illusion that the African customs recorded by many anthropologists is

any sort of guide to Africa's past. But they also need appreciate how much invented traditions of all kinds have to do with the history of Africa in the twentieth century?" PDF; Eric Hobsbawm and Terence Ranger 1983

KGOTLA; HOUSE OF WORDS IN BOTSWANA

KIROLERO; HOUSE FOR ALL IN INDIGNOUS BUGWERE – Ancient African Concepts and as you witness so from pages 80 – 83

Who is Imitating Who ...

Abrahamic civilization important decision-making buildings surrounded with African Spirituality Icons.

Who is Imitating Who?

"Interestingly from our point of view – inversion of traditions is the use of ancient materials to construct invented traditions of a novel type for quite a novel purpose. A large store of such materials is accumulated in the past in any ancient society and an elaborated language of symbolic practice and communication is always available. Sometimes new traditions could be readily grafted on old ones. Sometimes they could be devised by borrowing from the well supplied warehouses of official ritual symbolism and moral exhortation – religious and princely pomp, folklore, and freemasonry (itself an earlier invented tradition of Great Symbolic Forces) ... **Eric Hobsbawm and Terence Ranger PDF 1983**

Dr. John Henrik Clarke Said It Best;
"At What Point Are We Going To Stop
Imitating Imitators? You're Imitating
Someone Who Is Imitating You."

In vain do we seek tranquillity in the desert;
temptations are always with us; our passions
represented by the demons never let us alone. Those
monsters created by the heart, those illusions
produced by the mind, those vain spectres that are
our errors and our lies always appear before us to

seduce us; they attack us even in our fasting or our mortifications, in other words, in our very strength.

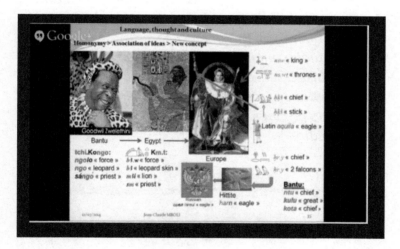

Who is Imitating Who?

... ("Eric Hobsbawm and Terence Ranger 1983; refers to modern societies and that includes, the regions of Europe and Nordic as Traditional Societies. The object and characteristic of traditions in those societies, including invented ones, is seen how inconsistency or invariance show off. The past, real or invented, to

which they refer imposes fixed (normally formalized) practices, such as repetition. In modern societies, rituals are traditions! In short: rituals in modern societies are responses to novel situations which take the form of reference to old situations, or which establish their own. But in most cases these traditions are the rituals commonly invented, constructed, and formally instituted, emerging in a less easily traceable manner within a brief, and dateable period, a matter of a few years perhaps – and establishing themselves with great rapidity") …

Who is Imitating Who?

When you look at Initiation of human organization, be it paternity, sovereignty, or Rights of Passage. These Rights of Passage always take you back if you are to go forward. At the foundation of every Rights

of Passage is a Ceremony that relates to Early Man in Africa where it all began. For indigenous Bugwere, contemporary Africa must go back and start as in "Sankofa" go back and get it, if you are to go forward.

Moreover, of course that is where we find contemporary Africa, today! Some people so very mistakably want to convince themselves the Rituals and Shrines in Africa are useless stuff, that has less function. Therefore, there is no Reason to go there. Why take us back in African Civilization?

Listen to Cheikh Anta Diop he has something important to share with you –

"The only salvation is direct knowledge. No laziness can exempt us from this effort. One must absolutely obtain direct knowledge. With equal training, truth triumphs. Train yourself. Arm yourself with science to the teeth. And seize your cultural heritage. Or drag me through mud when you get to that direct knowledge and find that my arguments are inconsistent"; **Cheikh Anta Diop**

- Abraham: the father of the so-called Holly Bible 2000 BCE ... wrote his book basing on Indigenous Africa Spirituality and beliefs in the African Nile Valley to get the skills right.
- The Persians 525 BCE went back to African Nile Valley to get the skills right.
- Alexander 333 BCE the Greco/Romans with Julius Caesar 50 BCE
- The Arabs in the seventh century.
- The Turks in the sixteenth century.
- The French with Napoleon and then the English at the end of the nineteenth century.
- Nevertheless, it would long continue to initiate the younger Mediterranean peoples; Greco/Roman among others into the
- enlightenment of civilization from the source; Africa in Antiquity.
- Throughout antiquity as well as the modern world, Africa remains the classic land where the contemporary world goes on pilgrimage to drink from at the fountain of scientific, religious, moral, and social knowledge, the most ancient knowledge of mankind will forever acknowledge; Africa origin of civilization – **Myth or Reality? Cheikh Anta Diop 1973.**

What do Africanists argue?

The Kybalion

"THE ALL IS MIND – THE UNIVERSE IS MENTAL"

This principle embodies the truth that "all is Mind". It explains that THE ALL (which is the Substantial Reality underlying all the outward manifestations and appearances which we know under the terms of

the "Material Universe"; the "phenomena of life"; "matter"; "Energy"; and, in short, all that is short, all that is apparent to our material sense) is Spirit; which is unknowable and undefinable, but which may be considered and thought of as Universal, Infinite, Living Mind? *"Unknown writer ...*

Amadou Hampate Ba (1981:170)

Let me point out, though, that at this level the terms 'speaking' and 'listening' refer to realities far more vast than those we usually attribute to them. It is said: 'The speech of Maa Ngala [the Creator] is seen, is heard, is smelled, is tasted, is touched.' It is a total perception, a knowing in which the entire being is engaged. In the same way, since speech is the externalization of the vibrations of forces, every manifestation of a force in any form whatever is to be regarded as its speech. That is why everything in the universe speaks: everything is speech that has taken on body and shape.

PR AA MERYIBRE KHETI Teachings to son MERIKARE c. 2100 BCE

Be skillful in speech, that you may be strong; [///] it is the strength of [///] the tongue, and words are braver than all fighting; none can circumvent the clever man [///] on the mat; a wise man is a [school] for the magnates, and those who are aware of his knowledge do not attack him. [Falsehood] does not exist near him, but truth comes to him in full essence, after the manner of what the ancestors said.

- Copy your forefathers, for [work] is carried out through knowledge; see, their words endure in writing. Open, that you may read and copy knowledge; (even) the expert will become one who is instructed.

After God is Dibia, Vol. 1 NOTES: by John Umeh 1997

If the assistance of the brave is appealed for at the war monger's place, the brave would take up his shield and amour and so it is fundamental that the Dibia must know the true name and pronunciation thereof of the herbs, roots, animals, birds, fish, reptiles, stones, minerals, stars, liquids, gases, soils, spirits, Deities, days, time of day, ages, periods, phases, places, sites, World ages, numbers etc., connected by the Universe, Dibia's words, *Ogwu*, and so on. My father was very insistent on this, I still remember a heated a heated argument he once had with Ikegbe Dunu allas Ogbukambakwe Onumba who was one of the great *Dibias* in my hometown and died in 1953. My father asked him to name the various herbs he Ikegbe, had assembled for fashioning *Ogwu*. He succussed in naming about a half the log and then held the remainder together and pronounced them as **Oghata na ibiom Ogwu** (which literally translates "chaotic and miscellaneous herbs for making *Ogwu*").

My father objected and insisted that for any herb or root or unit for making *Ogwu* to be potent and do its work efficiently and as required, you must call its true name and tell what it normally does and instruct it on what you want it to do in *Ogwu* under preparation.

Of Water and Spirit August 2010: Video Lecture by Malidoma Patrice Somé

At Minutes: 1: 11, 20 +++

... To be able to break it down into pieces, is what is called the discursive part and then there it was called the Melodic part ... any person who speak(s) is singing. There is a way in which you can determine the frequency of your verbal rendition, and there is a specific *frequency that you Must stay within to trigger the opening of another World.* it is not like a sentence that you can say anyway you would like, and then it would happen. No, and by the way, it is dangerous to say it the wrong way; something else might happen.

You might get zipped out of there. That is why I think that you know the Dagara peoples are very smart, they leave all that to only the people who have gone through Initiation, the people who learn how to control. And whereby there are many verbal keys like this. For example, there are (is) the one that can make you completely invisible, it can even make you invisible to the camera ... **by Malidoma Patrice Somé 2010.**

Sobonfu Somé

"When indigenous people talk about spirit, they are basically referring to the life force in everything, for instance, you might refer to the spirit in an animal, that is, the life force in that animal, which can help us accomplish our life purpose and maintain our connection to the spirit World. the spirit of a human being is the same way. In African tradition, the human is also seen as a spirit who have taken the form of a human so that the spirit in human body carry a purpose in /nTr/. Spirit is the energy that helps the human to connect in / nTr/ if we must see beyond the racially limited parameters. And in that way Ritual comes into play to help us in connecting with our ancestors. Ancestors are also referred to as spirit" by **Sobonfu Somé 1997**

What is spirit what is ancestors?

Sobonfu Somé 1997 argue; Ancestors in the next life are spirits. And the spirits in the realms of the spiritual world are spirit" –

But I like this one from the Roman-Catholic teaching that – they worship the Holy Spirit? They pray in Temples, Church, or Mosque ... but where is the difference? Spirit is spirit, whether Holly Spirit or Ancestor spirit, spirit is spirit, Kirolero is Temple or Church or Mosque because the place you kneel or humble yourself to pray to your God or Creator, is a Spiritual place.

Ancient Africa teaching about spirit ↔ ancestors ↔ spiritual world –

- The butterfly that hovered around you today, that was me.
- The feather that fell at your feet this morning, that was me.
- The sharp light that struck your eyesight the other night, that was me.
- The twinkling of your lower or upper eyebrows now and then, that is me preparing you to be aware, something bad, or good is due to happen in your life.

I am still around, guiding you to believe in the past, the present, therefore work hard for the future, you are infinite.

Argument –

Who is Imitating Who?

It is important for Africans to recover from erased memory of knowledge-of-self

And that should bring us to our communal knowledge so that Africans themselves will record what they say, write it down guided by fetching methodology and as Cheikh Anta Diop quoted on page 91 above. Not only, compare Ranykemet language with sister languages spoken in contemporary Africa and assemble the gathered information in community libraries in rural Africa. And that is to say; "Principles of Building Local Libraries in rural Africa. The other question is, how can I do this? Well, short answer is start from indigenous Africa languages spoken on your mother-knee, combine with primary studies in "A Beginners Introduction to Ranykemet also known /shw. mdw. nTr/ bring in the old French, old English etc to compare with ancient Africa languages and civilization, no more doubt about it anyways.

Moreover, there are also steppingstone books in this endeavour. The book titles start with the title; Principles of Building Local Libraries in Rural Africa followed by the book title; Mother Language Our Common Good. Followed by book title, Ancient Africa Culture Icons and Symbols as theory books to guide your field work. There are also examples of field work under these titles: "A Quest for the History of Bugwere Community", "Introduction to History of

A'bo Bwiisonkere Clan" and "A Day in Indigenous Bugwere Community".

Together these are simply steppingstones to fetching methodology from mother language our common good in ancient Africa. You can easily go on peer video review here –

- YouTube video review here: Well – come to SCLERA; A Sage Philosophy Presentation – to you today, besides, why SCLERA?
  27th March 2021 Event - YouTube

Rebirth of knowledge –

a Sankofa, go back to the source of birth of knowledge to get the Skills Right – Myth or Reality; Cheikh Anta Diop 1973.

Custom/common law must not be confused or interchanged with 'tradition' Here are some good examples of what a tradition

Here are some good examples of what a tradition is: •
The wig and gown the judge wears in court is a
tradition not a custom: a critique of Julius Malema. •
Napoleon sitting on the Pharaonic Throne is a
tradition not a custom: a critique of Julius Malema.
"'Tradition' in this instance is the institutionalized;
the ritualized, surrounding their substantial action;"
Eric Hobsbawm and Terence Rangers; PDF –
inversion of traditions 1983.

What do Africanist say?

If you listen and study Africanists, you get to
understand Africa is where Early man to establish
society spent very long time and advanced to modern
societies and into the period of our lives; the 21st.
century. So, for those people so far stuck up in
popular culture and behaviours that they would
rather let African spirituality be buried instead of
studying and understand that they are indeed lost? Is
indeed, the reason this book inspires you to get the
clear reason why you need to look for knowledge of
self in African spirituality.

Africanist here above mentioned; they ingrain your
understanding of spiritual world, and the evidence of

striking pieces of evidence with God; that there is, in fact, meaning to the ancestors ↔ spirit and ↔ God. In his book, Africanists are talking with you ...

Sobonfu Somé, author, teacher –

In her own words, Sobonfu Somé teaches us that; in her indigenous community; the Dagara nation of West Africa, women are valued as the source of the world's wisdom. They are valued as dreamers, as diviners, as the backbone of the community, the core of human survival. But what can the teachings of this indigenous cultures reveal to us about Women's Wisdom?

Sobonfu Somé, author, teacher, and the first woman empowered by the Dagara elders to impart their teachings in the period of our lives, Sobonfu Somé invites you to peer into a world where people remain closely connected to nature, their ancestors, and spirit, and to learn how to use powerful rituals to restore balance within yourself and with those around you. Secrets of the Dagara Storytellers Sobonfu Somé, whose name means "keeper of the rituals," was raised in her small village and sent by her elders to continue her education in the United

States. With Women's Wisdom from the Heart of Africa, Somé shares authentic spiritual teachings of her tribe that were formerly handed down only within the circle of Dagara village life. These teachings are founded in Africa worldview that honours animals, plants, and trees as our elders, and human beings as the newcomers. From this **revered relationship with the natural world**, we learn how-to live-in unity with our environment, and create a deeper connection with spirit. Discover Your True Gifts and Offer Them to the World Through Ritual and

Celebration. That will be *"eimerela, eimerela, eimerela – no'olusagaluko lube o'munssi ya Kibbumba".*

Then the question becomes; "in your indigenous view"; how do you find this connection to spirit? ... as for Africa Cradle of Multiple Civilizations, Rituals in the Spirit of Kibbumba the creator is the Gateway; distilling the essential practices of the spirit in the human body, Sobonfu Somé shows you how to check in with spirit to receive guidance, observe the sacred spaces of your home, harness the energy of the elements, strengthen your relationships, create balance in your professional life, and much more. Become concerned with the question; "what are your peculiarities, yet a common value in humans"? "How and why, you must exhaust the purpose of your communal knowledge", because you were not born for no purpose? Become concerned about the question; why were you born, and why were you born in that exact community or circumstance? These questions are asked of every born child confused of the whereabouts of his or her ancestry etc. Now, you have the chance to explore the questions to discover your inimitable gift as a child of human intellect.

Africa, home to early man –

Early man worked for his place in nature, created spirituality and rituals. Discover that the humans are spirits in human body form. Sobonfu teaches vividly about the spirit forms in the human body and the spirit in animals' body form. The female is council of women to initiate growth and change in a community, how to relate to your life cycles and honour them as times of grace, beauty, and immense energy; management; leadership as seen through the sense of Africa polygamist with his wives; the titles they inherit — a different way of using your power. How to create a Shrine for all in the courtyard to call to mediated in moral to the divine. Your unfiltered intuition—a guide you can always trust, "Call" in the spirits of the elements to create balance and harmony. Reclaim your ancestral lineage to learn who you are and what are your greatest strengths visible and invisible power—tapping into your own sacred energy. How to use grief and mourning to restore, renew, and regenerate your spirit. Draw upon your dreams to guide, support, and encourage yourself and others. Ritual is key to connecting with spirit and with the people you care about Several hours of rituals, reflection, and stories to immerse yourself in the footprints of Early man happened to image in Africa Cradle of Civilization and expand every spiritual be suitable.

Reaction and feedback to Rituals –

- Mike Prazen from South Africa commented – African Healing Rituals makes a lot of sense ... this is also common Ritual in some parts of southern Africa we still practice it ...just that

Christianity has mixed other people's minds and that part of the practice has been termed (devil) by the Abrahamic civilization yet they prove to be copy-cuts of African Spirituality.

- Johannes Motloung of Sweden commented –
  The colonial school curriculum coerces us to like and adopt to culture and tradition that we do not even know and understand that is why we are confused in contemporary society.

- No Wahalla in Jamaica commented –
  My Great Grandfather was arrested for obeah in Jamaica for doing this Ritual ...

- Jameel Sani of Nigeria commented –
  It is still practiced here in the northern part of Nigeria

- Morris I Nyamweya Omosa of Kenya commented –
  How I love to read more about our history! I wish I had powers to bring back golden days

-

- Kathy Whitman commented –
  So, this is the basics of therapy and spiritual healing, if you ask me …

- Mark Jesty commented –
  Hot cups are very effective, I use this method for Trapped nerves

- Higgins Gerard reaction –

The Way Forward

Join Africanists in the struggle to pull African Classic Studies please out of school corridors –

The aim-goal here is – become concerned about Questions like; every other continent of this world, worship God of their civilization, except Africa leave behind African religion to reach for worship of other civilizations? These are not questions to be brushed away.

Become concerned why is it said "Africa Cradle of Civilization" nonetheless, Ancient Africa history was pulled out of your school Teach yourself African languages plus teach yourself the surviving ancient Africa language to tap into your Africa Ancestral knowledge ... take basic /shw. mdw. nTr/ studies to understand where Africa is coming from, teach yourself where Africa should be if you are to Pass Down Ancestral Africa Knowledge Responsibly ...

There are affordable starting points or steppingstones; find on-line studies in the written down language; Ranykemet. Teach yourself at your own pace and at affordable price. Teach one to teach another.

Who is imitating who?

Every person is born with a different level of intelligence. This could never be changed. Yet through learning experience, take a step back to go forth, you can gain wisdom regardless of the intelligence level you were born with. So, in the period of our lives we should step back into Ancient Africa civilizations, follow them through if we are to move forward.

Fetching methodology from Mother Language in Ancient Africa –

You do not need to like and be liked by everyone. However, you need to act on human dignity even if you do not agree ... "A Day in Indigenous Bugwere" is Just a steppingstone to fetching methodology from mother language in antiquity. The omission of Ancient Africa History in the School Curriculum of our era, was not brilliant idea? "A Day in Indigenous Bugwere" inspires you to become part of the team to advance traditional libraries to modern society – showing concerns to pull away the dark cloud over Ancient Africa History disoriented from contemporary Africa history."

You may argue; contemporary Africa is safe without knowledge of Ancient Africa history. But that is not what the principle: Africa Cradle of Civilization was written for.

Share the knowledge that there is fulfilment of what the principle: Africa Cradle of Civilization is idea written down for mankind, not just for a few selfish minds.

Community libraries – the Elders of new age?

Old age or grey hair is not a sign of wisdom. If anything, it is a sign of honour (splendour). Logically, as we age, we are supposed to learn with life experience and know better. But we all know that it is not always the case. Not all know as we ought to. Old age doesn't equate to wisdom. The lessons to learn from a day in Indigenous Bugwere and "ask old woman" is not judge by appearance. The glory of the old is their strength. But it is not all the oldies with wisdom. There are young people who are wiser than some old ones. In the same way, just because a person is old doesn't mean he or she is wise. But, sometimes

Those new ages who created racism and corruption and invasion of indigenous cultures clearly was not a good idea So, those new ages clearly created bad things. But like the elders say, Saga the answer from this or that place, and share that information. Be aware of the Elders advice, so that you shall not be misled, so that racism and corruption come to a holt. Having beard or grey hair is not a sign of wisdom any more than having degrees or books signify intelligence. Wisdom is proved by our action. Be practical. Every day is school day. If you hide true history to save your face, history eyes are on you.

Key words –

1. Incentive to study Indigenous Bugwere
2. Indigenous Bugwere Time Management Plan
3. Communal Knowledge
4. The role of African Spiritual Philosophy
5. Bugwere Reserved relationship with nature; Ritual
6. Preserved old ways of African society
7. Green growth opportunity we want

Suffix

In Indigenous Bugwere Time Management is
important for communal knowledge. In the 21st
century, contemporary Africa is at the hour of the
cockcrow; Africa is ready to get out of colonial school
dogma. Contemporary Africa will no longer sleep in.
Africa has risen with the weapon of determination,
you must admit Africa has risen by the jaws of
consciousness that has begun to spread daily and
intensively, removing the cloud of colonial school
curriculum. a curriculum that was purposely written
to hide African history from contemporary Africa and
the World. Time tells, and so has 21st. century come
for Africa to take back her glory and touch the crown
of Africa Ancient Knowledge this time round that will
be in the local libraries and museums in all
indigenous communities.

About the author

The author is indigenous Bugwere history enthusiastic and admirer of the work of termites of the anthills. Moreover, living in the community is like that, fold-up your sleeves, prepare to work with community" aim from your local history to promoting community with goal for tomorrow. Get out of your history subconsciousness, be conscious of the work by your hand shall pass down to the next generation written down and assembled in your local libraries and museums. Be aware, some of it may pass down condensed in oral literature. That is fine.

The author is convinced that using the pictures, quotes etc., in this book is good idea because too much written work without pictures to show, coerces the reader to imagine, moreover sticking with the Colonial School Curriculum which teaches contemporary African history disoriented from Ancient African history anyway.

Printed in Great Britain
by Amazon

39491119R00066